Countries of the World

Australia

by Michael Dahl

Bridgestone Books

an Imprint of Capstone Press

Bridgestone Books are published by Capstone Press
818 North Willow Street, Mankato, Minnesota 56001
Copyright © 1997 by Capstone Press
All rights reserved
Printed in the United States of America

Library of Congress Cataloging-in-Publication Data
Dahl, Michael.
    Australia/by Michael Dahl.
    p. cm.--(Countries of the world)
    Includes bibliographical references and index.
    Summary: Discusses the history, landscape, people, and culture of the country of
Australia.
    ISBN 1-56065-521-6
    1. Australia--Juvenile literature. [1. Australia.] I. Title.
    II. Series: Countries of the world (Mankato, Minn.)

DU96.D3   1997
994--DC21

                                        96-50163
                                         CIP
                                          AC

Bridgestone Books wishes to thank the library at the Embassy of Australia for their help with
this project.

Photo credits
Flag Research Center, 5
FPG, 7, 19; Geelong, 9; Bibikow, 17
Root Resources/Hubbell, 11
Kay Shaw, 21
Unicorn, 5, 13, 15

Table of Contents

Fast Facts

Name: Commonwealth of Australia
Capital: Canberra
Population: 18 million
Language: English
Religion: Anglican, Roman Catholic

Size: 2,996,200 square miles
(7,790,120 square kilometers)
Australia is almost as large as the U.S.A.

Crops: Wheat, barley, and sugar cane

Maps

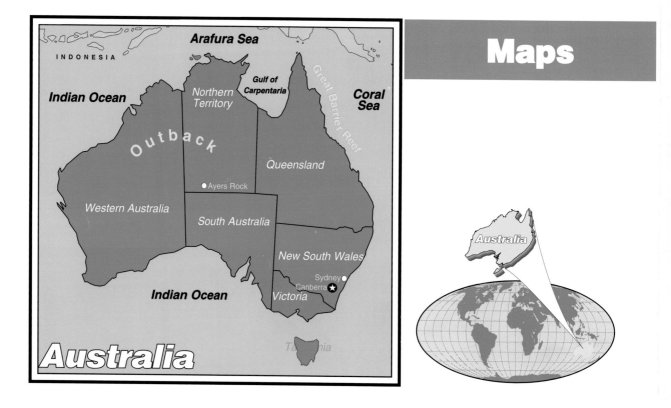

4

Flag

Australia's flag has the United Kingdom flag on it. It is in the upper-left-hand corner. This is because Australia once belonged to Great Britain. The rest of the flag is blue with six white stars. Five of the stars stand for the Southern Cross. The sixth star is called the Commonwealth Star. It stands for the six states and two territories of Australia.

Currency

Australia's currency is the Australian dollar. One hundred Australian cents equals one Australian dollar.

One Australian dollar equals about 80 U.S. pennies.

The World's Largest Island

Australia is called The Land Down Under. This is because it is south of the equator. The equator is an imaginary line. It is halfway between the north and south poles.

Australia is the only country that is also a continent. Australia is the world's smallest continent. But it is also the largest island in the world. Australia is the sixth largest country, too.

The middle of Australia is covered with deserts. Australians call this area the Outback.

Ranchers, miners, and groups of Aborigines (ab-uh-RIJ-uh-neez) live in the Outback. Aborigines are native people of Australia. They lived there before European settlers arrived.

The middle of Australia is covered with deserts.

The School of the Air

In Australian cities and towns, children have schools that are like North American schools. Many schools require students to wear uniforms. Australian children attend school from ages five to 18.

In the Outback, schools are different. Children who live there are too far from the city. They cannot get to school. So they listen to teachers on television or radio.

The radio school is called The School of the Air. Students listen to the teachers talk on radios. They talk into the radio and answer the teachers' questions. Tests and homework are sent through the mail.

Many schools require students to wear uniforms.

Bush Tucker, Australian Food

Bush Tucker is the name for traditional Australian food. Damper is flat bread cooked on an open fire. Billy tea is a drink. It is cooked in a pot on a fire. Mutton is a common meat. Mutton is meat from sheep.

Seafood is also a popular Australian food. Fishing boats catch fish, crayfish, and prawns for food. Prawns are shrimp.

For many years before Europeans arrived, Aborigines found their food all around. They still hunt kangaroo, catch fish, and eat berries and plants. Sometimes they eat insects.

Billy tea is a drink cooked in a pot over a fire.

Kangaroos and Koalas

Kangaroos are one of Australia's most famous animals. They carry their young inside warm, furry pouches.

Kangaroos eat herbs and grasses. They have powerful hind legs and a strong tail. They can leap great distances.

Koalas live in Australia, too. They look like little bears with sharp claws. Their claws help them climb the branches of trees.

Koalas live in trees. They eat up to two pounds (about one kilogram) of leaves a day. Koalas sleep for 20 hours a day.

Wild camels live in Australia, too. Herds of them wander around the Outback.

A koala's sharp claws help it climb trees.

Australians Outdoors

Australians like to be outdoors. They swim, fish, sail, and ski. They ride bicycles, horses, skateboards, and surfboards. They cook outdoors on barbecue grills.

Australia's national summer sport is cricket. It is played with a bat and a ball. Australians are very excited when they play cricket against the English.

Off the coast of Australia is the Great Barrier Reef. It is the world's largest coral reef. Coral is made of hardened remains of small sea creatures. The reef is more than 1,200 miles (1,920 kilometers) long. At the reef, people dive, wade, and watch fish.

People dive, wade, and watch fish at the reef.

Sydney and Road Trains

Sydney is Australia's largest city. One-fifth of all Australians live there. Sydney has Australia's biggest harbor and tallest buildings. It also has 40 beaches.

The Sydney Opera House is one of the world's most famous buildings. It is built near the harbor. The building is shaped like seashells.

Australians travel between cities by car, train, or plane. There are few roads in the Outback. Most ranchers use small planes or trucks to get around.

Giant trucks, called road trains, travel the lonely Outback roads. Road trains travel all day and night. They carry livestock and supplies from the Outback to ports.

The Sydney Opera House is shaped like seashells.

The Outback

The Outback is full of interesting sights. The most famous is Uluru (oo-LOO-roo). It is the largest rock in the world. The sun makes Uluru look different colors throughout the day. Sometimes it looks like a huge, glowing, red whale.

The Bungle Bungle is made up of hundreds of rocks. The rocks are shaped like giant beehives.

Some of the Outback deserts have red sand. Australians call the area Red Center.

There is a wet season in the Outback. Birds, frogs, and animals gather at water holes when it rains.

Uluru is the largest rock in the world.

Australia Day and Corroboree

Since Australia is south of the equator, the seasons are different from North American seasons. June and July are winter months. December is in the middle of Australia's summer. Families often go to the seashore for vacation in December.

January 26 is Australia Day. This day celebrates Australia's first European settlement.

Aboriginal celebrations are called corroborees. Men and boys paint their bodies and dance. They move and make sounds like animals of the Outback.

At corroborees, Aborigines also make music. They use their voices and clap sticks together. Sometimes they play a didjeridu (did-jer-ee-DOO). This is an instrument made from a hollowed branch.

For corroborees, men and boys paint their bodies.

Hands On: Make ANZAC Cookies

Australian and New Zealand soldiers from World War I (1914-1918) were called ANZACs. In 1915, more than 8,000 soldiers died in a famous battle. Australian children remember the soldiers by baking ANZAC cookies.

What You Need:

1/2 cup melted butter
1 cup flour
3/4 cup sugar
1 cup oatmeal
3/4 cup coconut flakes
1 tablespoon maple syrup
1/2 teaspoon baking powder

What You Do:

1. Set the oven at 325 degrees.
2. Mix all the ingredients together in a bowl.
3. Use a teaspoon of dough for each cookie. Place them on a greased cookie sheet.
4. Bake the cookies for 15 minutes.
5. Let cookies cool for 10 minutes before eating.

Learn to Speak Australian

barbecue grill	barbie	(BAHR-bee)
great, excellent	bonzer	(BOHN-sah)
a chicken	chook	(CHOOK)
real and good	dinkum	(DINK-um)
to complain	grizzle	(GRIZ-zl)
see you later	hooroo	(HOO-roo)
a good friend	mate	(MATE)
thank-you	ta	(TAH)

Words to Know

Aborigines (ab-uh-RIJ-uh-neez)—native people of Australia who were there before European settlers

corroboree (kor-OH-boh-ree)—an Aborigine celebration

equator (i-KWAY-tur)—an imaginary line halfway between the north and south poles

Outback (OUT-bak)—a huge area in the middle of Australia that is covered by deserts and rocks

Red Center (RED SEN-tur)—the place where Australia's four deserts meet

road train (ROHD TRAYN)—a giant truck that brings things to and from Outback towns

Read More

Cobb, Vicki. *This Place is Lonely.* New York: Walker and Company, 1991.

Kelly, Andrew. *Australia.* New York: Bookwright Press, 1989.

Lepthien, Emilie U. *Kangaroos.* Chicago: Children's Press, 1995.

Useful Addresses and Internet Sites

Embassy of Australia
1601 Massachusetts Avenue NW
Washington, DC 20036

Information Center on Children's Cultures
332 East 38th Street
New York, NY 10016

Australia Online
http://australia-online.com/FUN.html

Explore Australia
http://www.aust.emb.nw.dc.us/map/html/ausmap.htm

Index